Cornelia Street

Mark Eitzel and Simon Stephens

T0371890

methuen | drama

LONDON · NEW YORK · OXFORD · NEW DELHI · SYDNEY

METHUEN DRAMA
Bloomsbury Publishing Plc
50 Bedford Square, London, WC1B 3DP, UK
1385 Broadway, New York, NY 10018, USA
29 Earlsfort Terrace, Dublin 2, Ireland

BLOOMSBURY, METHUEN DRAMA and the Methuen
Drama logo are trademarks of Bloomsbury Publishing Plc

First published in Great Britain 2023

A catalogue record for this book is available from the British Library.

A catalog record for this book is available from the Library of Congress.

ISBN: PB: 978-1-3504-0146-4
ePDF: 978-1-3504-0147-1
eBook: 978-1-3504-0148-8

Series: Modern Plays

Typeset by Mark Heslington Ltd, Scarborough, North Yorkshire
Printed and bound in Great Britain

To find out more about our authors and books visit
www.bloomsbury.com and sign up for our newsletters.

Cornelia Street had its world premiere at New York's Atlantic Theater on 20 January 2023 with the following cast and creative team:

Book	**Simon Stephens**
Music and Lyrics	**Mark Eitzel**
Choreography	**Hope Boykin**
Director	**Neil Pepe**
Scenic Design	**Scott Pask**
Costume Design	**Linda Cho**
Lighting Design	**Stacey Derosier**
Sound Design	**Kai Harada**
Music Direction	**Chris Fenwick**
Orchestrations	**John Clancy**
Music Contractor	**Antoine Silverman**
Production Stage Manager	**Jennifer Rogers**
William	**George Abud**
Jacob	**Norbert Leo Butz**
Philip	**Esteban Andres Cruz**
Misty	**Gizel Jiménez**
Daniel McCourt	**Jordan Lage**
Marty	**Kevyn Morrow**
Sarah	**Mary Beth Peil**
Patti	**Lena Pepe**
John	**Ben Rosenfield**

Cornelia Street

Characters

Jacob, *fifty-four, a chef*
Patti, *fifteen, his daughter*
Philip, *twenty-nine, a waiter*
Marty, *fifty-four, a restaurant owner*
Sarah, *seventy-four, a retired opera singer*
William, *thirty-seven, a taxi driver*
John, *twenty-eight, a computer scientist*
Misty, *thirty, a waitress*
Daniel McCourt, *fifty-two, an investor*

Marty's. A small, battered café on Cornelia Street in the West Village of New York City.

It's out of time. Out of fashion. Out of place.

Late spring to early summer.

Around the edges of the stage, surrounding the café, is a space.

It's like a space for the ghosts.

The actors who are not in the scene should populate the space. The musicians should populate the space. We can see the space around the edges and through the windows at the back of the restaurant. It is from this space that they sing and that the music comes. The music haunts the restaurant. It breathes into the café and out again.

Act One

Late spring.
The interior of Marty's Café on Cornelia Street.
A right-angled counter in front of a wine rack. A beer fridge. A spirit shelf.
A kitchen off behind the bar.

There are three booths and two tables angled around the counter.
There is a window.
A door leads to the street.
Another door to the back of the house.
The back of the house leads to an apartment upstairs where **Jacob** *and* **Patti** *live.*

The cast appears at various parts of the stage.

Jacob

When you go out tonight
We're your big destination
Where this weary nation goes
To eat

Philip

When you go out tonight
Just bring all your money
We have your milk and honey
Take a seat

Jacob / Philip

When you go out tonight
You wanna live
Just for one short night
You wanna live
The good life

Patti

Does your mother love to swoon
Does she like a darkened room
Did she show you the moon
Like it was her heart

Sarah
I have hundreds of shoes
I like cigarettes and booze
I'm impossible to refuse
Let me play a part

Jacob / Philip / Patti / Sarah
When you go out tonight
You wanna live
Just for one short night
You wanna live
The good life

William
You people are all fools
You never know the rules
You'll lose the family jewels
Unless you learn to fight

John
I slave night and day
Trade my soul for pay
No one cares if what I say
Is wrong or right

Jacob / Philip / Patti / Sarah / William / John
When you go out tonight
You wanna live
Just for one short night
You wanna live
The good life

Marty
Never say you're through
Though yeah it might be true
Lose your spirit and you'll
Be high and dry

Jacob
I always got a scheme
I always got a dream

You can't lose with a gleam
In your eye

Jacob / Philip / Patti / Sarah / William / John / Marty
When you go out tonight
You wanna live
Just for one short night
You wanna live – a good life

Jacob *is left on stage with* **Patti** *his daughter.*

Jacob   You lied to me.

Patti   It wasn't a lie.

Jacob   If there is one thing I can't stand, Patti, if there is one thing, I swear to God, it's people lying to me. The only way we can do anything is if we tell each other the truth.

Patti   Honestly, I don't know what you are talking about right now.

Jacob   I'm your father.

Patti   I kind of noticed that.

Jacob   There were things which I needed to know, and I didn't know them and the reason that I didn't know them was because you kept them from me. Emails I needed to reply to.

Patti   That's not my fault.

Jacob   Meetings I had to go to. Targets I needed to know about that had been established because of the mistakes you made.

Patti   Wow.

Jacob   Don't 'wow,' Patti. Seriously. The last thing I need from you is a 'wow,' Patti, you failed two of your finals! You know what that means, right? Your Guidance Counselor says you have one chance to re-take them, or you gotta take 'em again *next* year, on top of all your other classes. The rate you're going you ain't gonna graduate. You really want that, in this city?

Patti   What has this city got to do with anything?

Jacob   This city is unforgiving.

Patti   I don't think that's true.

Philip *enters to stock the fridge.*

Patti   Hey, Philip.

Philip   Hey, babe.

Jacob   I'm talking to you.

Patti   I can tell that.

Philip *works while they talk.*

Jacob   You got homework?

Patti   I've done it.

Jacob   You have?

Patti   On the subway.

Jacob   On the subway? I bet it is a towering academic achievement of the highest order.

Patti   You know you shouldn't be sarcastic to children, right?

Jacob   You know you should do your homework in a quiet stable place where you can do your best work to the best of your ability, right?

Patti   Like where?

Jacob   At the bar.

Patti   The bar?

Jacob   The bar.

Patti   Classy.

I've already finished it but since you asked so nicely, I'll check over it at the bar. How's that?

Jacob   That's great.

She gets her work out.

Patti   Ask Philip.

Philip   Ask Philip what?

Patti   Ask him what dicks they are at that place.

Philip (*as he leaves*)   Always with the 'dicks'.

He leaves. **Patti** *works as* **Jacob** *tries to talk to her.*

Jacob   You know what I realized? I was up all night thinking about this.

Patti   Thrill me.

Jacob   It's me as much as it's you. I need to be better for you. I need to inspire you.

Patti   Dad, are you okay?

Jacob   And that is what I am going to do. You watch me.

Patti   I am entirely baffled at this point.

Jacob   Like Daniel McCourt. Did I ever tell you about Daniel McCourt?

Patti   Er . . .

Jacob   He's a friend of mine.

Patti   You have a friend? That's cute.

Jacob   The time we spent together! The things we did! I ain't seen him in a long time. Now he, *he* is a man who has succeeded in this city. You know what he is thinking about? He is thinking about buying this place.

Patti   Marty's leaving?

Jacob   Not just the restaurant. The whole freaking building. Marty heard last week. The owners are going to sell.

Patti   They are?

Jacob   The second the realtors put it on the market me and Marty are gonna go and see him.

Patti   Where are we going to go if this place gets sold?

Jacob   This is what I'm saying to you. We'll bring him back here. Show him what we've done to the place. He's in real estate now. It's what he does.

Patti   Nice.

Jacob   You know how he succeeded?

Patti   I don't really know who he is, Dad, so I guess –

Jacob   By telling the truth.

Patti   In real estate?

Jacob   And being better than anybody thought he could possibly be.

So now? You watch me. From today. The place is changing. I'm changing. You're changing. We're all changing.

Patti   Seriously? Is this what it's gonna be like now? One lousy parent-teacher meeting, and you're going to talk to me like this?

Jacob
    I hated school so what can I say
    Stared at the clock for the whole damn day
    But I won't let you throw your future away
    You could own the world

    The rats are killing the rat race
    So everyone's wearing a rat face
    Don't let them put you in last place
    You must own the world

    A real estate king like Dan McCourt
    Partied all night but held down the fort
    Always found something good to snort
    You could own the world

You could be a doctor that everyone begs
For her miracle knife that everyone says
Makes beautiful faces purses, arms and legs
You could own the world

Or a scary lawyer with three big phones
Billable time in all the best time zones
Squeezing dry the international stones
You could own the world
You could own the world

Or be an astronaut seeing stars
Beaming down to TVs over bars
Hanging with Elon Musk on Mars
You could own the world
You must own the world
You must own the world

So I'm saying this with a loving heart
Don't be clever just be smart
Get As in science get As in art
And you will own the world

Never know when is enough is enough
One mistake they slam that door
You can't haggle or call their bluff
You give everything and still owe more

You must own the world
Or you have nothing
Or you have nothing
Or you have nothing
Or you have nothing

Philip *re-enters with more stock.*

Patti   Did you never think that the reason I won't make twelfth grade is because I'm not as good as you think I am?

Jacob *reels a touch. Recovers.*

Jacob   It's not that she's not smart, Philip.

Philip   I know she's smart.

Jacob   The stories she writes. Have you read the stories she writes? What was that one?

Patti   Dad don't.

Jacob   *The Ghost Heart*. Was that what it was?

Patti   I don't believe this.

Jacob   Go and get that story

Patti   No.

Jacob   *The Ghost Heart* it was called.

Philip   Nice title.

Patti   You are so embarrassing.

Jacob   It was about a man and he had –

Philip   A ghost for a heart?

Patti   Shut your mouth, Philip.

Jacob   The words she uses. Her vocabulary.

Philip   I'm sure.

Jacob   How in hell is this kid flunking out of high school with a vocabulary like that.

Marty *enters.*

He has the food order form in his hand.

Marty   Iberico ham? Seriously?

Jacob   It's the best ham in the world.

Marty   You use ham as a filling for a freaking omelet.

I'm not going to Balducci for a filling for a freaking omelet. I'll put it on the CityFood Order.

Jacob   It's not the same.

Marty   Clearly, it's not the same. It's $3,000 dollars cheaper.

Jacob   Don't exaggerate.

Marty   An ounce. When did you change the order, Jacob?

Jacob   Today. I changed the order today.

Marty   And Palacios chorizo?

Jacob   It's for pizza. It's Spanish. From Seville. It's the best chorizo you can get in this city. A proper chilli sauce. A great chorizo. The right crust. I want to start stretching myself.

Marty   Why?!

Jacob   We're gonna show Dan. If you increase the quality, you can increase the price. You increase the margins.

Marty   There are two ways of making money in this business, Philip.

Philip   Don't get me involved in this.

Marty   You can make astonishing food that people will pay astonishing mark ups for. And sell astonishingly expensive booze.

Jacob   This is what I'm talking about.

Marty   Or you make good food cheaply. And sell lots of booze.

Philip   Or bad food. Very cheaply.

Patti   And a shit tonne of booze.

Jacob   Patti!

Marty   I like you, Jacob.

Jacob   I like you too.

Philip   I like both of you.

Marty   But you're busting my balls here. Sorry, Patti.

Patti   That's okay.

Marty   We need new wine glasses by the end of the month.
I got to get some plumber out to check the flush in the
restroom because that thing is not smelling right.

Philip   Honey, I noticed.

Marty   You know how many reservations we got tonight?
We got one. Table for two at six. They're going to the
freaking theater. They gotta be out by seven. After that we've
got nothing. We're averaging two walk-ups a night. And
they're the same freaks who've been coming here since I
even *thought* about coming to the city.

Jacob   Well maybe if our menu was better –

Marty   The rent on the lease is brutal enough even if the
owners don't sell.

Jacob   That is not an issue.

Marty   XL Realty bought up fifteen units in the past two
months. They bought up Po.

Philip (*his heart breaks*)   Po?!

Marty   They are unforgiving motherfuckers. Sorry, Patti.

Jacob   It's not an issue because we're going to show Daniel
what we can do.

Has he written back to you?

Marty   Even if he does, the margins on this place hold my
testicles, effectively, they effectively hold my testicles in a
vise. And every time you order something like that you turn
that vise just a little bit tighter.

Philip, **Patti** and **Jacob** *all take a second to take in this image.*

Philip   Sweet.

Sarah *enters. All scarves and glamour and old cigarette stains.*

Marty   Evening, Sarah.

Sarah   Darling.

Marty Forgive me. I just need to go hold my head in a bucket of freaking ice. For a very freaking long time.

Sarah Oh, I know that feeling.

Marty *leaves.*

Jacob Hey, Sarah.

Philip Hello, Sarah.

Sarah Good evening, gentlemen of my heart. Patti my love.

Patti Hey.

There.

Jacob What?

Patti Done it.

Jacob Already?

Patti You wanna see?

Jacob What is this?

Patti Quadratic equations. They all good you think?

Jacob I honestly have no freaking idea.

Sarah I can check them.

Patti What?

Sarah I can. Mathematics is something of a forte.

Patti Seriously?

Jacob *triumphs.*

Jacob Here.

Sarah Excellent. Excellent. Excellent. Excellent.

Patti Ha.

Philip *smiles and leaves.*

Jacob Ha what?

Patti   I'm taking a moment. And then I'm going to my room.

Patti *smiles at* **Sarah** *and sticks her tongue out at her dad and leaves.* **Jacob** *brings* **Sarah** *a glass of pastis.*

Jacob   She's failing her classes.

Sarah   She is?

Jacob   She hid letters to me, from her teachers.

Sarah   Which shows initiative.

Jacob   She forged my signature.

Sarah   And skills in calligraphy.

Jacob   I'm being serious, Sarah. I don't know what to do about her.

Sarah   You don't need to do anything about her.

She has the gift.

Jacob   She has the what?

Sarah   Whatever happens to this place, she will be fine. She is graced.

Jacob   She may well have 'the gift', Sarah. It's a shame she just can't apply that 'gift' to her fucking classes.

You should have heard what they said about her last night.

I'm busting my balls here, and she's going to repay me by screwing up from here to kingdom come.

Sarah   She won't do that.

Jacob   She will, Sarah. The way she's fucking going.

Sarah   You'll see.

Drily lifting events she believes to be factual.

She's going to live until she's eighty-two surrounded by people who love her. She'll live in four different countries in two different continents. She'll raise two beautiful children and live to meet her great grandchildren.

Jacob *allows this news to settle in.*

Jacob
Sarah
I know you'd never lie to me
I believe everything you say
Is it true that you can see
Beyond the god damn milky way

Sarah
Just tell me she'll be happy
That's the only hope I can't lose
Tell me please she'll be happy
She's the hope I can't refuse

Tell me everything will be all right
'Cause everything must be all right

Against the truth
Fortune tellers fight
Tell me everything'll be all right

Sarah
Wake me tell me
What I keep
Headline is everything will go
Wake me so I'm not fast asleep
Dreaming through my favorite show

Everything must be all right
Tell me everything'll be all right

William *enters the bar.*

He is wearing a cowboy shirt.

William   Jacob.

Jacob   William.

William   Sarah.

Sarah (*coolly*)   Hmm.

William   How are you sweetcheeks?

Sarah   I'm fine. Thank you so much for asking.

Jacob   That's quite a shirt you've got there, William. It is quite a thing.

William   1948 Levi Strauss original.

Jacob   It's a thing.

William   Two hundred and forty dollars.

Jacob   Fuck.

William   From a vintage store in Rockaway.

Jacob   For a shirt?

John enters. *He has a kind of sing song 'hello'. It's his signature.*

John   Hello.

Jacob   Good afternoon, sir.

William   How the hell does he get to be called 'sir?'

Jacob   Because he's a respectable man.

William   He's a milk boy for a tax evader, how is that respectable?

Jacob   It's more respectable than dealing –

William   Dealing what? Cab rides? Is that what you were going to say?

Jacob   Yes, it was.

William   I hope it was.

Jacob   It was. Don't listen to him.

John   It's no problem.

Jacob   What can I get you?

Philip enters.

John Can I get a ham omelet and tomato salad and a Brooklyn IPA.

Jacob Hey. Would you do me a favor?

John A favor?

Jacob I went to Union Square this morning.

John You did?

Philip Oh Jesus Mary and Joseph.

Jacob Don't tell Marty. I got some porcini mushrooms. I'm gonna put them in an omelet. You wanna taste?

John I mean. I kind of like a simple ham omelet. It's the main reason I come here. Because it's simple.

Jacob Will you try it?

John Okay. Sure. I'll try it.

Marty *enters.*

Jacob *leaves to set about making the omelette.*

Marty Hey, man.

John Hello.

Marty William.

William Chief.

Marty How's life in the cab trade? Is it busting your chops as badly as Mr Iberico-goddamn-ham-for-an-omelet-side-order is busting mine?

William It's getting kind of intense out there.

Marty Now that is true.

William It is not possible to do anything in this city any more other than work. We don't have time to think. We don't have time to eat.

Marty We don't have time to sleep.

William   We don't have time to have a drink.

Marty   There is always time to have a drink.

William   I mean I kind of like it. It's got a kind of honesty to it. I don't want to come across as one of those half-cocked quinoa-assed liberals that spend half their time complaining about capitalism and the other half counting their money. But Jesus. Nobody speaks to anybody anymore.

(*To* **John**.) That's your fault.

John   Excuse me?

The music for 'New York is a Magic Trick' starts.

William   People get into my cab.

John   I don't really see how that's my fault.

William   They stare into their screens. The whole ride. Pay with their card. Wish they were in a goddamn Uber so they didn't have to speak to anybody at all. Get out. The spirit of the Ferryman in the River Styx of this city has been decimated by our friends of the 9th Avenue Google HQ.

William *sings 'New York is a Magic Trick'.*

William
  Ask me and I'll tell you
  Which card you will pick
  It's a real good trick
  I always make my own luck

John   I don't really understand what you're talking about exactly.

William
  You flip a coin hoping
  Somehow it'll change your life
  It flashes like the knife
  That turn you into a schmuck

John   None of this makes any sense to me.

William

New York is a magic trick
That doesn't care which card you pick
Claps its hands and from thin air
The crap you're living for

This city only wants your heart
Wants to take the deepest part
Robs you blind but still you want
To give it even more

John   Ah. I see.

William

In this city you need to be rich
To be free
And then you can talk about liberty
Something to be bought or sold

Gotta have money
Gotta scratch your itch
Also hunger's a bitch
Don't be unlucky or old

As the scene continues occasional chords from 'New York is a Magic Trick' punctuate and underscore the scene from the ghost world.

Jacob *returns and presents the omelet.*

Everybody watches.

John *tastes it.*

Everybody watches.

John   Now that – is a great omelet.

A chord.

Marty *leaves.*

John *takes his phone out to photograph the omelette.*

A chord plays.

John   Can I ask you something, Jacob?

Jacob   Ask me anything.

John   How long have you been a chef?

Jacob   Twenty-eight years.

John   That long? Gosh.

Was it always the thing you most wanted to do with your life?

Jacob   Yes, it was.

John   I envy that.

Jacob (*calling*)   You hear that, Patti?

Patti *enters.*

A chord plays.

Jacob   I'll tell you.

A chord plays. **Philip** *enters. Slightly appalled to be hearing this story again.*

Jacob   I was eight years old. I was born in Jersey City. There was a butcher on Newark Avenue. I have no idea what his name was. He had this shop. In the window of the shop were these hams. Hams as big as –

William   A pig.

Jacob   No. Not a pig. I mean yes a pig. Obviously a pig. But. I'd never seen anything like them. The colors. And one day this guy. He gave me a cut. Just a sliver. And the way it melted in my mouth.

Philip   I've had things melt in my mouth on Newark Avenue.

Patti   Ha!

A chord.

Jacob It was a taste that transported you. From the middle of Jersey City to a place the likes of which you could never imagine. And I thought if I could do that. With food that I made. Well that wouldn't be a bad way to live a life. And you wanna know something?

John What?

Jacob You wanna know who used to shop there? In that butcher's? On Newark Avenue, Jersey City?

Patti Dad, please.

John I have no idea.

Jacob Bruce Freaking Springsteen.

Philip Oh God.

John Really?

Jacob It's true.

Sarah Don't get him started.

John The Boss?

Jacob The very same. He used to buy his bacon there.

A chord.

He came in here one time.

Sarah You don't say.

Patti Here we go.

Jacob What?

Marty *enters.*

Marty What's he doing?

William He's doing the Bruce Springsteen story.

A chord.

Marty How many times?

Jacob   Came in here. Sat in the corner. He had an omelet too! He chose a mushroom omelet.

A chord.

He sat. Ate every bit. Said it was great. They were his very words. Looked at me. 'That was great man.'

John   Gosh.

Jacob   Stood up. Left twenty dollars on the table. Walked out the door.

William
   We all want that magic trick
   We all want the card we pick
   The house wins and for your sins
   Sells you the finest dope

   The city only wants your soul
   Makes damn sure you pay the toll
   The thug you trust sells you the
   Dust of 400 years of hope

Jacob   There was a time this place was packed you know. This place. 1975. Everybody ate here.

John   Were you here in the seventies?

Jacob   No, I moved to New York in 1980. I've been chefing this place for Marty since 1994.

He's let me and Patti sublet this place since she was born.

John   I imagine it's changed a certain amount in that time, hasn't it?

Jacob   Some things have. Some things haven't. Same people owned the building since 1923.

Sarah   Until now, I found out last week.

Jacob   Even if they sell it doesn't matter. Me and Marty are gonna go and see Dan McCourt. Did I ever tell you about Dan?

Philip 'Dan'?

Jacob He made a ton of money in real estate after 2008.

Marty He never called him 'Dan'.

John Really?

Sarah He used to be such a handsome man.

Marty Nobody ever called him 'Dan'.

Jacob He's what you would call 'dependable', Patti. He wouldn't mind about Marty subletting the apartment to us. Especially when he sees the food I can make here.

Sarah There used to be more bums.

William More bums. More winos. More junkies. More gunshots. More actual murders in the actual street. But you know? It still carries a certain panache.

William *leads the bar in a chorus of 'New York is a Magic Trick'.*

William

New York has no magic trick

But there's no other card to pick

Makes pride a boast

Your soul a ghost

Throws the rest away

But I never want to go

This magic place is all I know

But it got sold

And hearts are cold

So we all go away

Jacob *pops out to the kitchen.*

Misty *enters.*

She is wearing a fur coat and sunglasses and a green silk dress. She is carrying a huge suitcase.

Philip   Good evening. Welcome to Marty's. Come and take a seat.

What can I get you?

Misty   Is Jacob Towney here?

Philip   Jacob? Sure. He's –

Jacob *comes back.* **Misty** *catches her breath when she sees him.*

Jacob   I'm Jacob Towney.

Misty   Don't you remember me?

Patti   Dad? Who is this?

Misty   I'm Misty.

Jacob   Oh my God.

Sarah   Stars and stripes.

William   Oh Jacob, you dark old dog.

Marty   Misty?

Jacob   Misty? Sweetheart?

Sarah   She's Laura Hickman's girl.

Marty   Oh holy shit on a horse.

Jacob   Misty? I've not. I don't. How are you? You look –

Misty   Have you got something to drink?

Jacob   To drink? Sure. Of course. I mean of course. I mean, what would you like? Sit down here.

Misty   No, I wanna stand.

Philip   What would you like to drink?

Misty   I want some water. I walked from Grand Central. I had no money for the subway.

Jacob   Jesus Christ.

Misty   I had no money for anything and I heard you were still here.

Jacob   It's been fifteen years.

Misty   Yeah. Yeah. It has.

Patti   Dad? Who is this?

Misty   You must be Patti. They called you Patti, right? Is what I heard. Your dad kind of met your mom when he was supposed to be married to my mom so I kind of thought that it must be you.

Jacob   Misty –

Misty   You're exactly the age now that I was back then.

Philip   Some water. I got you ice and lemon.

Misty   Mom died.

Sarah   Laura died?

Misty   Three weeks ago. Emergency One. Kingston, New York. I got on the train and I lay her ashes and came down here to say hello.

Jacob   Jesus, Misty.

Marty   What happened to her?

Misty   Her liver rotted. Her kidneys rotted. Her heart dried up.

William   I know that feeling.

Jacob   I don't know what to say to you.

Misty   She owed a hundred and seventy-five thousand dollars to the hospital. We didn't have it. They took our place. My mom was a wreck all her life. And it was because of you.

Jacob   That's not fair.

Misty   The things you did to her.

Jacob   I tried to help your mom. The whole time I was with her.

Misty (*to the tune of 'One More Night'*)
  If this dump had a story
  It faded like glory
  Now its on a shortlist to
  Disappear

Jacob   From when you and her first walked in here.

Misty
  God it still smells like piss
  Something I didn't miss
  For this relic not a
  Single tear

Give me some money.

Jacob   I don't have any money.

Misty   Give me some money or I swear to God I don't know what I will do.

Jacob   Misty. I am sorry about Laura.

Misty   Give me some money or I'll rip your goddamn face off.

Jacob   She is not my responsibility any more.

Misty   I'll burn this place down.

Marty   What the fuck?

Misty   I'll smash every glass and every plate in this whole shithole.

Marty   Jesus shit, girl.

Jacob   I'm not responsible for the things that happened to your mother.

Misty   She died like a broken piece of wood.

Jacob That's not my fault.

Misty It so is.

Philip *brings her some tea.*

Philip Here.

Misty What's this?

Philip I made you some tea. You wanna sit down? Drink it.

She looks at him for some time.

They watch her decide whether or not to drink the tea.

Misty
   Let me be the night
   Watch me quietly fall
   Listen to the sirens calling
   For blood

   Let me be the night
   Watch the city close
   A life I never chose
   The flood

   Just for one short night
   I wanna live
   Just for one short night
   I wanna live

The lights fall.

Act Two

The café.

Three-and-a-half weeks later.

Early evening.

The place is being set up for the evening sittings.

Misty *and* **Jacob**. *He brings her a plate of food.*

Jacob   Here.

You didn't have any lunch. I saw.

Misty   I wasn't hungry.

Jacob   You look kind of pasty.

Misty   Pasty? Shit.

Jacob   It's huevos rancheros.

I started making the guacamole myself. There are chillies you can get from a market in Queens. I read about it. In *The Times*. Went out there.

You're welcome. Is there anything else I can get you?

Misty   I'm good.

Jacob   You good for dough?

Misty   For 'dough'? Sure.

Jacob   You can stay as long as you want. You know that, right?

Misty   It's been a month already, Jacob.

Jacob   Three weeks.

He watches her setting the tables. She doesn't interrupt her work to talk to him.

There's something I wanted to ask you.

She carries on working.

You said you lay her ashes, I was thinking I could –

Misty   I put them in the Hudson.

Jacob   Right.

Misty   I couldn't think of what else to do with them. Got off the train at Grand Central. Headed to the River. Found a nice spot just south of the NYPD tow pound. Threw her in. Walked here. It wasn't one of the great days.

Jacob   She liked the river.

She looks at him. Incredulous at his attempt to soften the shitness of this.

Sorry. That must have been hard.

He watches her work.

We let each other down. Me and Laura.

He watches her work.

Before she really started with the drinking.

Misty   Don't blame her.

Jacob   You should have seen her. And when you two were here. Watching the way she played with you!

That changed. You may not remember it. She hid bottles of Scotch in every room in the house so she could always get to one when nobody was looking. She thought I didn't know. She took two half pints to bed with her every night because if she didn't she'd wake up in the night shaking. I didn't want to divorce her. I tried not to for years. Maybe I should have. Before I found my own fucking way of fucking things up.

She looks at him.

I had this idea. I think I could paint the room. For you and Patti.

Misty   Paint it?

Jacob   It hasn't been painted for a long time. I can try and get the money together from somewhere for, like, some paint and do it properly.

Misty   I have no idea how long I'm going to be in the city for.

Jacob   No. I know. Sure.

Misty   I don't think I'm the kind of person you want hanging around here for too long, Jacob, you know what I'm saying?

Jacob   But if you want to. You can.

She looks at him.

Looks away.

Misty
   When I was small
   I was quiet and shy
   Before you could breathe
   I'd say goodbye

   I'm too much for anyone

   When I was a child
   I was always sent out to play
   And I'd just sit there on the steps
   Sometimes I'd wait all day

   I'm too much for anyone
   For anyone
   For anyone

   I swear I was a good girl
   At least I gave it my best try
   But it's pissing in the wind
   Like trying to deal with her
   When she was high

   All this nostalgia's a treat
   But hey cash will be sweet

I'm sick of saying sorry
All the time

It's too much for anyone
For anyone
For anyone
For anyone

Philip *enters, puncturing their intimacy.*

Philip   Cute.

He is about to step out again when **William** *enters from the street.*

William   Hey.

Philip   Hey.

Jacob   Hi, William.

Philip   You sitting at the bar or you wanna eat?

William   No. No. No. I'm good.

Jacob   Can I get you a drink?

William   No thank you.

There is some time. Nobody knows what to do if **William** *is just going to stand here.*

Philip   Is there anything I can –

William   Can you go outside?

Philip   Outside?

William   Let me know if there's anybody out there. On the street.

Philip   Anybody?

William   Anybody.

Philip *leaves.*

Jacob   You okay?

William *nods. Waits.*

Philip *comes back.*

Philip   Nobody.

William   Nobody?

Philip   On the whole street.

William *nods. Thinks.*

William   That's fucking great. That's fucking great. That's fucking great. That's fucking great. I'll see you later.

William *leaves.*

The three look at each other.

Philip   What the fuck?

Jacob   I have no idea. I gotta get prepping.

Jacob *leaves.* **Philip** *and* **Misty** *work setting up the bar for a while.*

Misty   He looked terrified.

Philip   Yeah.

They work. As they talk the restaurant gets more and more prepared for their evening diners.

Philip   You okay?

Misty   Oh. You know. You?

Philip   Oh yeah. You know.

Misty   You had any auditions this week?

Philip   No.

Misty   Nothing 'coming in'?

Philip   No.

Misty   Not managing to get in any 'rooms'?

Philip   No.

Misty   Shit.

Philip   Yeah.

They work.

Philip   How's it going for you here?

Misty   It's okay. I'm okay.

Philip   This job working out for ya?

Misty   For now.

Philip   He's thrilled you're here.

Misty   He keeps talking about having me 'back'. Which is just plain weird.

Philip   I like him. When I first got here. I was kind of, you know, living la vida loca. He straightened me out. I was fucking myself up.

Misty   Honey, I been there. Done that. Sang that song. Played a fucking encore.

He looks at her.

Philip   Yeah?

Misty   One day at a time, you know?

Philip   Can I ask you, have you talked to Jacob about that?

Misty   Why would I talk to Jacob about it?

Philip   Coz of Patti.

Misty   What's Patti got to do with anything?

Philip   You're sleeping in her room.

Misty   I have nowhere else to go.

Philip   I don't want to be a stone cold prick here but she's the closest I've got to a sister.

Misty   Jesus, Philip.

Philip   Jesus, Philip, what?

Misty   Jesus, Philip, give a girl a goddamn break.

He looks at her.

Philip   You stocked the dairy fridge?

Misty   Yes, I have.

Philip   You filled the wine rack?

Misty   Yes, sir.

Philip   You gonna fold me some napkins?

Misty   I'm gonna fold you hundreds of the fuckers.

Philip   We got five reservations in tonight.

Misty   How is this happening?

Philip   They like the new food. And how 'it counterpoints the lo-fi interior'. Is what one of them told me. They said it felt 'authentic'. Just keep 'em drinking.

Misty   Always one of my specialties.

She starts folding napkins. He refills the bar.

Philip   It must have been hard, coming here.

Misty   No.

They work.

Misty   You know what was hard? Watching my mom's heart break over that dumb chef fuck. That was hard. Leaving here. Moving to Kingston. That was hard too. Living so close to every other apartment in the block it was like we could hear the snoring through the fucking walls. One time, I got home, I was fifteen years old and some fucking thief had shit in the bathtub.

They work.

Misty   The first time I stole anything I stole two diet pills and a pack of Virginia Slims from my mom's purse. She cried when she found out. That was hard. Coming here to speak to him? Less so.

They work.

Philip   I'm just watching his back.

They work.

Misty
    When you look all you see
    A woman of breeding and class
    I act like some trash celebrity
    No matter what I get a pass

    Since I walked in
    One thing is clear
    If you wash up
    You wash up here

    Here's what I know
    Leave before they make you stay
    So when I leave I'm a star
    I shine so bright they wanna pay

    I know what it means
    To disappear
    You drift into the waves
    And wash up here

    No speeches please
    Maybe a big Bronx cheer
    I drifted with the breakers
    And washed up here

They work.

Philip   I like that.

Misty   What?

Philip   Being quiet.

They work.

Patti *enters. She is dressed up. Done something pretty with her hair.*

Patti She here yet?

Philip Not yet, sweetheart.

Misty You look beautiful.

Patti You sure?

Philip Here.

He readjusts something ever so slightly. Her hair. Or something about her dress. A finishing touch.

Perfect.

John *enters.* **Misty** *kind of lights up when she sees him. She doesn't notice herself doing it.* **Philip** *does. So does* **Patti**.

Philip Hey, handsome.

John Hello, Philip. Hello, Misty.

Misty Hey, John.

Patti Call me when she gets her.

Patti *leaves.*

Misty How you doing?

John I'm good. I'm very good. It's good to see you.

A touch of a moment between **John** *and* **Misty** *that is interrupted when* **Jacob** *enters.*

Jacob Good evening, sir.

John Hello, Jacob.

Jacob Can I make a suggestion?

John Absolutely.

Jacob The ravioli. I made the pasta this morning. The venison is from Hunts Point. In the Bronx. Don't tell Marty. I got up this morning and went and got it myself. It will melt on your tongue.

John   That sounds, er, amazing.

Jacob *leaves to set about preparing the ravioli.*

He comes in and out of the kitchen as he cooks and pitches his restaurant at the same time. He pops in.

Jacob   John.

John   Yes, sir.

Jacob   You're a citizen of some intelligence.

John   I don't know what to say about that.

Jacob   I had an idea.

Philip   Everyone's got one.

He pops back to the kitchen. **Philip** *and* **Misty** *finish the preparation of the restaurant.*

Jacob *(off)*   About this place and what we could do to it if Dan takes the building.

He pops in.

And now that Misty's back.

Misty   What?

He pops back into the kitchen.

Jacob *(off)*   We could specialize. We could turn this place into a restaurant with a theme. You wanna know what the theme is?

Philip   Thrill us all.

He pops in.

Jacob   Eggs.

John   Eggs?

Jacob   The egg is a beautiful thing. Every egg contains a life waiting to come to be.

He pops out.

They are a little baffled by his pitch and his popping in and out.

Nobody knows what to say.

Philip *tries but can't.*

Philip   I –

Jacob (*off*)   We only do eggs. Everything egg based. Omelets. Huevos rancheros. Deviled eggs. Egg pasta if we're cheating.

John   Scotch eggs.

He pops in.

Jacob   Yes!

He pops back to the kitchen. Calls from off.

Eggs Benedict. Eggs Florentine. Eggs Royale.

He pops in.

What do you think?

John   I think it's very interesting.

Misty *leaves.*

Jacob   I think I can just get Marty on board. Raise awareness. You could help me.

John   I could?

Jacob   Because one of my ideas was that I could write a blog. An egg-based blog.

John   I could certainly help you build a site.

Jacob   'Build a site.' Wouldn't that be a thing?

You show me how to 'build a site' and I'll show you the perfect way to make an omelet.

He pops back to the kitchen.

And hey!

John   What?

He comes back.

Jacob   You should ask her.

John   Ask who.

Jacob   Misty. You should ask her out. Take her to the movies. Take her for something to eat. Go for a, a, a walk. Get out of here.

John   Jacob I don't know why you think I want to take Misty out.

Jacob   I noticed the way you look at her. Your face.

John   My face?

Jacob   It kind of lights up.

John   She's very striking but the thought has never even crossed my mind.

Jacob   I'm saying it should.

Sarah *enters as* **Jacob** *serves* **John** *his ravioli.*

He photographs it before he eats.

Sarah   Good evening, gentlemen of my heart. How are we?

Jacob   We're well.

Sarah   How's the world wide web?

John   I'm not sure it's possible to attribute an emotional condition to an interconnected network using standardized communication protocols. Not yet. Maybe one day.

Sarah   I worry about you. The Googlers. Your company is eating up my city.

Patti *enters. As though expecting somebody that wasn't* **Sarah**.

Patti   Oh.

Hi, Sarah.

Sarah   Hello, darling. You look pretty.

Patti   Thanks, Sarah.

Philip   I promise I will call you when she gets here.

Patti *leaves.*

Misty *returns. She brings* **Sarah** *a glass of pastis.*

Sarah   Thank you, darling.

Jacob   How is it? The ravioli?

John (*he thinks*)   It's very, very good.

Jacob   And the venison?

John   It's toothsome.

Jacob   Did you get a good photograph?

John   I did.

Jacob   Did you Instagram it?

John   I will.

Jacob   Did you ever think about investments?

John   Excuse me?

Jacob   You must have made some money? In your time. Working there.

John   Some. I guess.

Jacob   How much? No. You don't need to tell me that. Did you ever think about investing it? It's the intelligent thing to do with money.

Coz if things go how I think they could we could be looking for investors. And I admire you.

John   Thank you.

Jacob   And your work and your success. I am a man who admires success.

Some men envy the success of others. I admire it. And if you wanted you could come in with us?

John I'm not sure I completely understand –

Jacob If Dan buys the building you could invest in this place.

Misty Jacob.

Jacob I've been thinking about this for some time now. It could save my skin.

Misty *turns away from him.*

Jacob What?

John *considers the proposal.*

John I don't think that would be a good idea.

Jacob What do you mean?

John I don't want to invest my money in your new idea for the restaurant.

Jacob Why not?

John It's not really an idea that appeals to me.

Jacob Are you kidding?

John No.

No, I'm not.

I feel like I should say I'm sorry.

Philip You shouldn't.

Philip *leaves.*

John I'm not trying to be rude.

Jacob No. It's not that. I just think you're missing an opportunity.

John   It's not an opportunity because it's not an absence that needs filling. I don't think food service sector is an intelligent target for any investment in this city. It's a saturated market Anyway, I don't want this place to change. I like it how it is. It makes me feel like I'm at home.

Jacob   Can I tell you something?

John   Please.

Jacob   You should take your money more seriously.

John   I do.

Jacob   Because it won't last forever. Believe me, I know.

Jacob *leaves.*

Sarah *is alone with* **Jacob** *and* **Misty***.*

The music starts for the 'Dead Boys of New York'.

John   I didn't mean to let him down.

Misty   You didn't.

Sarah (*to* **John**)   Look at you.

John   What about me?

Sarah   The way you look at her when you think nobody's looking.

John   That's er – Excuse me?

Sarah   You have the eyes of a poet.

John   Thank you.

Sarah   And you're wasting them. We live once John, my love. We can't waste our natural talents.

Misty   Ha!

Sarah   I bet you're the type of man who wishes he could buy a girl flowers but somehow doesn't quite dare.

Let me tell you. Women like flowers.

She sings her song for the 'Dead Boys of New York' to **Misty** *and* **John***.*

Sarah

   You just sit down
   And hold your tongue

   The crazy lady
   Has something to say
   There's never time when you're young
   And you don't see it 'til time slips away

   I was crazy 'bout a man with crazy big plans

   He scribbled them all over his walls

   We laughed for weeks we never had to speak

   He was high and happy I loved it all

   He lived on West 14 and then it was a scene

   All night the screams of the damned

   He was a leaf on the water who hated his mother

   Slept with a beer in his hand

   Loving an angel is
   Bad for your liver
   For them nothing gets old

   But the love of an angel nothing is better
   In their arms you dont feel the cold

   I left him in the dawn his TV always on
   My mom was yelling there's more to life

   I never told him I loved him a fling it meant nothing

   And I'm too smart to be someone's wife

   Then for twenty long years no one ever saw my tears

   There were lovers but I was alone

   And in life you must act

   There's no turning back

   Or regret's the only thing you'll own

I loved him when
I was a singer
But singing standards got old
Nothing's better than pills and liquor
But when you sing
You don't feel the cold

A poet's eyes
Should not have this much pain
They should be pleased with themselves
And a little dumb

So get the damn flowers
And throw off the chain
I'm beginning to think
You're no fun

Jacob *returns.*

Jacob *looks at* **John** *who can't look back at him or really at* **Misty***.*

John   I have to go.

Jacob   Yeah?

John   I liked the ravioli tremendously. Thank you. I'll see you tomorrow. I'm sure.

He leaves. **Jacob** *watches the door as though he's going to come back and change his mind. He doesn't.*

Jacob   Well we got five reservations tonight. I should get ready.

Sarah *sips.*

Patti *enters.*

Patti   What time did Mom tell you she was getting here?

Sarah   Crystal's coming?

Patti   She's taking me out.

Sarah   We haven't seen Crystal for a while.

Patti She missed last month. She had a holistic retreat. What time?

Jacob She said about six.

Misty *looks at* **Patti**.

Patti What time is it now?

Jacob Seven-thirty.

Misty *exits. She tries to touch* **Patti** *as she does but* **Patti**'s *having none of it.*

Patti Did you tell her about my exams?

Jacob No.

Patti You better not. I don't need to her to know yet. I'll tell her in my own time.

Jacob I didn't, Patti.

Patti I bet she's just running late.

Sarah I hope so, my love.

Marty *enters.*

Marty Jacob, what's in the ravioli?

Jacob Braising beef.

Marty Don't fuck with me.

Jacob Venison.

Marty Where did you get the venison from? Where did you get the goddamn venison from, Jacob?

Jacob It's delicious.

Marty Where from, Jacob?

Jacob Have you tasted it?

Marty I haven't, no. But I have seen the receipts. Shit, Jacob. You have to stop doing this. Daniel wrote to me.

Jacob   He did?

Marty   He's interested in checking the place out. He wants to see some figures. He's interested in its viability.

Jacob *looks at him for a beat. Considers this.*

Philip *enters.*

Jacob   What did I tell you?

Marty   He will want to see everything. He will be thorough.

Jacob   He's a thorough man.

Marty   So if he thinks I'm not making any money because you're spending it all on bullshit sausage patties from a god damn market in Queens, he will know precisely what to fucking do.

Jacob   Come on, Marty, taste it.

Marty   I don't need to taste it.

Jacob   John loved it. Didn't he?

Marty   You don't think. All these years. You keep fucking, sorry Patti, spending money I don't have. This is my place. If we fuck this up, I will lose everything. And then *you* will lose everything. And you won't be able to cook a venison fucking ravioli because you won't have a fucking kitchen. You will be on the fucking streets. You will have nowhere else to go.

Patti   You shouldn't talk to him like that.

Marty   I shouldn't what?

Patti   At least he's trying to do something with this place. Not just sitting on his ass complaining.

Jacob   Patti, please.

Patti   You talk to him in a way that is fucking, sorry Marty, mean. It's really fucking, sorry Marty, irritating.

Jacob   Patti, quiet.

Patti   No.

Jacob   That's enough.

Patti   Don't tell me to be quiet. He talks to you like that in front of me and you just let him. You don't say anything. You don't even try to stick up for yourself? All you can do is tell me to be fucking quiet?

Patti

I only tell you what
You want to hear
Easier to lie
Than make it clear
I sit and listen to you talk all day
And what do you say
You say nothing

Who cares who cares
Who gives a damn
Tomorrow burning down
You make eggs and ham

What exactly in your story
Makes you proud
That you fought and fucked
With the music too loud

You do nothing
You do nothing
You do nothing
You do nothing

You're my world
You're my dad
But you had a future
That I'll never have

Your dancing days
Are dead and gone
Still play air guitar
At every goddamn song

The trouble is
I used to believe
You could pull magic
From your sleeve

The past is a shadow
Where you cling
A rising tide
Takes everything

You do nothing
You do nothing
You do nothing
You do nothing

The party's over
Where will you all go
You've run out of moves
Spent all your dough

You'll still be groovin'
When the ship
Goes down
A rude surprise
When you start to drown

We do nothing
We do nothing
We do nothing
We do nothing
We do nothing
We do nothing
We do nothing
We do nothing

She leaves.

Jacob   I'm sorry, Marty.

Marty   Yeah?

Sarah   Crystal was supposed to be here.

Jacob   She's stopped replying to her emails. She's stopped replying to my texts.

Marty   Patti ain't the problem, Jacob. Patti's a bad ass mother fucker. I always like that in a woman. You're the problem.

William *enters.*

Philip   Welcome back.

William   Fucking pricks.

Marty   Hey, William.

William   Fucking arrogant disrespectful obnoxious fucking little pricks.

Marty   How are you, William? I'm good thanks, Marty; how are you?

Marty *exits.*

William   Out there. Strutting around. Pricks. Little pricks. Violent. Nasty pieces of shit. Children. That is no exaggeration They are children. They lack respect. For precedents. And territory. And status. Do those cunts, and I use the word deliberately, do those cunts have the slightest fucking idea who the fuck I am?

Jacob   You okay?

William   I'm good.

Philip   You don't sound good, sweetcheeks. You need me to go outside and have a look around for you?

William   You know what I need. I need a fucking Merlot. Help me take my mind off those juveniles.

Philip   Coming right up.

He fetches **William** *a Merlot and exits.*

Sarah (*to* **William**)   Are they pricks or are they cunts?

They hold each other's stare for a while.

Sarah   Hm.

She stands to leave.

I am going to kiss a brief goodnight to Patti and then I shall light out for the territories. (*To* **William**.) I hope the children calm down.

William   Oh they will.

She leaves.

Jacob *watches* **William**.

William   Quite a girl.

Jacob   Yes, she is.

William   She's good for Patti, huh?

Jacob   Yes.

William   How old is she?

Jacob   I honestly have no idea.

William   She has great tits.

Jacob   Jesus, William.

William   I don't normally like old people. They make me nervous.

Patti *enters.*

Patti   Hey, William.

William   Hey, Patti. How you doing?

Patti   I'm okay. Sarah said I should say a proper goodnight.

She gives her dad a reluctant kiss. But nevertheless, a kiss.

William   He still busting your balls about your exams?

Patti (*she looks at him before she answers*)   It's okay. They're important.

William   You know you have good kids, Jacob?

Jacob   Yeah?

William   You make good kids. Your girls. They're good.

Patti   Misty's his stepdaughter. He didn't make her at all.

William   No. But still.

I mean look at you.

Patti   What about me?

William   You're beautiful.

Jacob   Jesus, William.

William   What?

Patti   Dad!

William   I'm paying her a compliment here.

Patti *looks at* **Jacob** *and leaves.*

William   Kids, huh.

Where's Misty?

Jacob   She's out back.

William   She coming up here?

Jacob   She will be.

William   You trust her, Misty?

Jacob   Yes, I do.

William   Or is it just that she reminds you of her mom?

William *smiles. Takes a dab of coke.* **Jacob** *pauses in his work. Is he gonna scold him?*

Jacob   William.

William   Jacob.

Jacob   Can I get a bit of that?

Just to get me through.

William *considers him.*

William   You going back to 2004 again?

Jacob   No.

William   I heard all about *that* party?

Jacob   Never.

William   How much do you want?

Jacob   Not even a line. Just a bump.

William   I'd sell you a bag for like fifty dollars.

Jacob   I haven't got fifty dollars.

William   No?

Jacob   I haven't got fifty dollars, William.

William *thinks, smiles, gives him a dip from his bag of coke.*

Jacob   Thank you.

William   That's okay.

Jacob   You're a good man.

William   I'm really not.

Jacob   You know?

William   What?

Jacob   There's a lot about your life I envy.

William   You shitting me? You have no fucking idea.

Jacob   I came to New York when I was seventeen. I had all these ideas about how my life was gonna turn out. When I think about those ideas now, I don't know if I should laugh or shit. I had Patti. Two hundred and forty dollars on a shirt after that? Are you fucking kidding me? I work all the time. Seven days. End of the week I don't have two hundred and forty cents. I'm restricted. I'm trapped.

William   You really don't have fifty bucks?

Jacob   I'm not proud of it.

William   You know the defining characteristic of an island? There is always a shore.

Jacob   What the fuck are you talking about?

William   You have some opportunities in this place.

Jacob   ?

William   I spend time in a lot of the restaurants round here. A lot of the bars.

Jacob   You do?

William   I've been looking at this place for a while.

Jacob   I don't understand.

William   More of your customers use cash than in any other joint in the whole neighborhood. Is the thing that I have observed.

I could help you use that.

Jacob   Use it?

William   A cash-based business nowadays? You could use it to sell

Jacob   Sell what?

William   Shit, Jacob. What do you think? Little porcelain models of cute little puppy dogs with cute little eyes. Let's stop fucking about here.

Jacob   Oh.

William   I could sell you 2,000 dollars of cocaine right now for a thousand dollar advance plus a thousand dollars in one month's time. You'd make eight grand.

Jacob   Are you shitting me?

William   I'll package everything. I could put word out to let people know you were here. You'd be in effect a counter service. All you'd need to do is be ready to serve people when they asked you.

Jacob   No, William.

William   Six thousand dollars profit in a month.

Jacob   I'm a chef.

William   Sure. An artist. I know.

Jacob   How am I gonna get a thousand dollars?

William *looks at him.*

William   You can do the banking on this place, right?

If you're careful you bank ninety-five dollars for every hundred earned every day for three weeks.

You telling me you've not got a thousand dollars in this place right now?

Jacob   I am not going to steal from Marty.

William   He'd never suspect you.

Jacob *turns away from* **William**. *He is going back to work. He opens the till. He closes it again.*

Jacob   I have to get ready. We have five reservations.

William   Before he'd noticed you'd have paid it all back and got your interest and turned over a four hundred per cent profit. Buy all the vintage shirts you fucking need.

Jacob   No. No. No.

William   Its mathematics.

Jacob   No.

They look at each other.

Act Three

The café.

Early summer.

Night-time.

The debris of the end of the night is strewn. Chaos and clutter, and tables too tired to be cleared yet.

Marty *and* **Jacob**.

Marty *is dressing for a night out.*

Using the restaurant as a makeshift changing room. He checks his tie in the mirrors in the restaurant walls. **Jacob** *watches him.*

Marty   What time is it?

Jacob   It's ten after ten.

Marty   It's still hot.

Jacob   Yes, it is.

Marty   That was a busy night.

Jacob   Nine reservations and three walk ups.

Marty   Your freaking, your venison and your ravioli shit! Who knew?

Jacob   Me. I knew.

Marty (*testing his tie*)   How's this?

Jacob   It is good, Marty. It goes with your eyes.

Marty   What time you gonna get there?

Jacob   I'll give it another hour. Less. I swear. I gotta help Philip close the place up properly.

Marty   Daniel specifically said he wanted to see you. It's why he was happy to meet late. It felt like you being there was kind of like a condition of the meeting kind of bullshit thing.

Jacob   I ain't seen him in years.

Marty   He said to me that you were a 'fundamental part of the story of this street'.

Pause.

Jacob   Huh.

Marty   I told him I didn't know what the fuck he was talking about.

Jacob   'A fundamental part'? How do you like that?

Marty   He said that 'community matters'. That 'having somewhere to eat at the heart of a street in the heart of the neighborhood matters'. He said 'Authenticity has an innate market value of its own right now'.

I think if you're there, if you come, we can persuade him.

Jacob   I'll be less than an hour.

Marty   And put a goddamn jacket on.

Jacob   I will.

Marty   You wanna borrow a tie?

Jacob   I'm good.

Marty   The way it works is this: I make the argument. Based on the facts and the figures of the recent situation and projecting from that into the near- and medium-term future. He'll listen to me for my figures.

Jacob   Who wouldn't?

Marty   But he'll get sentimental when you're around. I promise you. You watch him.

Jacob   Nostalgic, is the word.

Marty   So you just gotta make sure you're there.

Jacob   I know that.

Marty   You can't let me down, Jacob.

Jacob   I won't.

Marty   The things they're doing round here.

Jacob   I know that.

Marty   They'll turn this place into a –

Jacob   They won't.

Marty   They will eventually. You just watch. Shit. It'll be some goddamn branch of something.

Jacob   A shop selling –

Marty   Precisely. It will be the branch of a shop selling –

Jacob   Bags.

Marty   Fucking bags. Or worse. It'll just be empty. It will be too expensive for a shop selling bags. It will be an empty unit. And somebody in Moscow or Abu Dhabi will have it as a place to dump their goddamn money.

How's Misty?

Jacob   She's okay.

Marty   Looks like she's staying, huh?

Jacob   I don't know.

Marty   Don't Patti mind her sharing her room?

Jacob   Not for now.

Marty   With her exams coming up? They're important, Jacob.

Jacob   Believe me. I know that.

Marty   It's good.

John   What is?

Marty   You having your children. I envy that sometimes. She remind you of Laura? Misty?

Jacob   All the time.

Marty   She has the same eyes.

Jacob   She does,

Some time.

Is Charlene confident about Daniel?

Marty   She doesn't want to talk about it. She's tired of the city. She has an idea about going home to Vancouver Island. And looking for whales. And kind of living there. With the goddamn whales.

Jacob   She's one hell of a woman. You're a lucky man.

Marty   Luck has precisely nothing to do with it.

Marty
    I hope you're good and ready
    It's time for some good news
    And here it comes
    Here it comes
    For days without worry
    For hopes you can't lose
    Here they come
    Here they come
    If there's a chance
    I'm gonna take it
    And if there's a chance
    I'm gonna make it
    Today I feel like superman
    Bulletproof and tall
    Here I come
    Here I come
    I'll keep the sky from fallin'
    I'm here to save us all
    Here I come
    Here I come

If there's a chance
I'm gonna take it
And if there's a chance
I'm gonna make it
If I'm offered a hand
I'm gonna shake it
Give me one chance
I know I'll make it

So I'm telling you this
In my most grown-up voice
Here it comes
Here it comes

The future is right now
You don't have a choice
'Cause here it comes
Here it comes

Gemma at The Bowery.

Jacob   East 3rd. I got it.

Marty   You sure you don't wanna come with me? I'm gonna jump in a cab.

Jacob   No. This place is a bit of a mess.

I'll get myself cleaned up. I'll text you when I'm leaving.

Marty   Do that. Don't let me down.

Jacob   I won't, Marty. I'll come the second we close.

Jacob *opens the door for him.*

Marty *leaves.*

Jacob *is alone.*

He thinks. He checks his watch.

He sends a text. He waits for a reply. There is none.

Jacob *goes to a dry goods cupboard behind his food counter.*

He opens it. Takes out a Tupperware box.

Opens it. It is full of bags of coke.

He takes one out.

He has absolutely no idea what to do with it. He has never felt more naïve in his life.

Philip *enters.* **Jacob** *puts everything away before he is seen.*

Jacob   Don't sneak up on me! Jesus!

Philip   I wasn't sneaking.

Jacob   You were. You do. You sneak up on people. You're silent. It's unnerving.

Philip   Pardon me for breathing.

Some time. They work cleaning up the restaurant.

Philip   I thought you were going with Marty.

Jacob *looks at him a beat.*

Jacob   I will. I'm going to. He said he didn't need me to come straight away.

Philip   Really?

Jacob   Said he's better on his own. Told me to hang here for a while. I'll go down for a drink to seal the deal.

Philip   Huh.

Some time. They keep clearing up.

Jacob   You're looking sharp.

Philip   I had an audition.

Jacob   An audition?

Philip   For a show. In Schenectady.

Jacob   Well that's good.

Schenectady, huh?

Philip   Playing a soldier.

Jacob *throws him a look.*

Philip   What?

Jacob   Nothing.

Philip   What?

Jacob   A soldier?

Philip *glares at him. Some time. Then they work cleaning up. Their work cleaning up continues through the rest of the act.*

Jacob   Philip.

Philip   What?

Jacob   Nothing. Don't worry about it.

Some time. They work.

Hey.

Philip   Hey.

Jacob   You know anybody who likes to – ?

Philip   What?

Jacob   You know, man.

Philip   I really don't.

Jacob   Party.

Philip   Party?

Jacob, honey, I have literally no idea what you are talking about.

Jacob   William gave me some coke to sell.

Philip   He did what?

Jacob   And if you knew anybody who might be interested in that then I could arrange to meet them. Not here. Somewhere else. Another time. But if, you know –

Philip   Did he give you some or did he sell you some?

Did he give you some or did he sell you some Jacob?

Philip
>   You stupid fucking bitch
>   You think you're getting rich
>   I may be 'funny' but
>   Honey I'm not a fool
>
>   All that money you will owe
>   Will never let you go
>   It'll chase you you like a
>   Turd in a public pool
>
>   Who do you think you are?
>   When have you ever had to pay?
>   Who do you think you are?
>   For this smile I fight every day
>
>   Most of us try
>   To slip on by
>   And evade the world
>   And its dirt
>
>   But when you walk this road
>   You become so cold
>   And everyone you touch
>   Gets hurt
>
>   Now you're New York's favorite joke
>   They'll all laugh until they choke
>   The funniest clowns think
>   They know the score
>
>   Are you really not aware
>   Or maybe you don't care
>   A lie is a stone
>   Dragging you to the floor
>
>   Who do you think you are?
>   What the hell did you do?

Who do you think you are?
I thougnt maybe you knew.

You became a ghost
Making toast
I shouldn't expect
You to see

This is my family
How could you lose me?
Without trust
We are lost

John *enters.*

Neither **Philip** *nor* **Jacob** *know quite how to react for a while.*

John   Hey.

Philip   What? Hey. Hey. Hey John. Hey. You're in late.

John   I know.

Jacob   We stopped serving food.

John   I know that. I come in here every day. I know what time the freaking kitchen closes.

Philip   You wanna drink?

John   Please.

Philip   Brooklyn IPA?

John   Brooklyn IPA.

Philip   You okay?

John   Yes.

Philip   You sure?

John   Just.

Philip   What?

Philip *brings* **John** *his beer.*

John   Sometimes the demands that my employers place on my imagination are more exhausting than people might ordinarily assume.

Philip   Believe me, honey. You have no idea.

John *drinks.*

John   I saw Marty getting into a cab on Bleeker. I thought you were going with him. I thought tonight was your big meeting.

Jacob   It is. I am. There's no hurry. I'm gonna join him when I'm done here.

Jacob *looks at* **John**.

Sarah *enters. She has a scratch on her forehead.*

Sarah   Good evening, gentlemen of my heart.

Philip   Hey, Sarah.

John (*his signature*)   Hello.

Jacob   What happened to your head?

Sarah   It's nothing. A silliness.

Philip   Did you fall?

Sarah   Not 'fall'. No. It wasn't a 'fall'. I'm not that old.

William *enters.*

Jacob   Man. Finally!

William   Hey, Jacob. How's it going, brother?

Philip *leaves.*

Jacob   I thought you said you were coming in about six. I was waiting for you.

I've gotta get out of here.

William   I'll have a Merlot, thank you Jacob.

Misty *enters.*

John   Hello.

She gives **John** *a smile but doesn't answer. She glares at* **Jacob** *before she talks.*

Misty   Hey.

Jacob   Hey.

Misty   How you doing?

Jacob   I'm doing good. I'm doing good.

Misty   Sweet.

Jacob   What's wrong?

Misty   Nothing.

Jacob   You going out?

Misty   I was going to go and read.

John   What are you reading?

Misty   I'm reading *Harry Potter and the Prisoner of Azkaban.*

John   A great book.

Misty   Yeah.

Misty *goes to leave.*

Jacob   William. I need a word. I don't have much time.

Misty *stops.* **Philip** *watches* **Jacob.** **William** *senses the atmosphere change. He loves it.*

William   I'm drinking my drink.

Misty *thinks. Approaches* **Sarah.**

Misty   Do you still sing?

Sarah   What?

Misty   When I was a girl. I think this is right. You used to sing. Operas. I used to stand outside your door and listen. That was you wasn't it?

Sarah   It was me.

Misty   Do you still do that?

Sarah   Not anymore.

Ever so gently **Misty** *touches* **Sarah***'s graze. Like ET healing a wound.*

Misty   I used to sing.

Jacob *is pulled away from* **William**.

Jacob   You did?

Misty   I taught myself the guitar. I sang. I tried to get into the New School one time. Move back to the city. Didn't work out. (*To* **Jacob**.) Life, huh?

(*Then back to* **Sarah**.) You were special.

Sarah   Not quite special enough.

Misty   But you sang concerts, right?

Sarah   I did. I sang in Toronto one time.

Jacob   I remember that.

Sarah   I remember you didn't come and watch me.

Jacob   I never fly. I hate the idea of flying in a plane. It terrifies me.

William   You're funny.

Jacob   Funny how?

William   You talk all the time about all the shit you're gonna do and the places you're gonna go and how you're gonna prove yourself to Patti and you're gonna prove yourself to everybody and you won't even get on a goddamn plane! You should just get over yourself, brother.

Jacob   Don't call me that.

William   I was merely positing an observation.

Sarah   You want to prove yourself to people? You should take me dancing.

Philip   Dancing?

Sarah   Sure. He's a magnificent dancer.

Jacob   Oh Jesus.

Jacob *throws himself even harder into cleaning up.*

John   Jacob is?

William   Jacob?

Sarah   It's true. We used to go dancing together. All of us.

Jacob   I don't have time for this.

Sarah   We used to go to the Studio.

William   Jesus. The Studio?

Jacob   I didn't.

Sarah   He did. He loved it.

Jacob   Fucking terrible clothes.

William   Get the fuck out of here.

Jacob   Terrible music.

Sarah   Nile Rodgers was always trying to get in. Liza Minnelli was there. What a woman. Farrah Fawcett, I saw. Jack Nicholson. Richard Gere. Sylvester Stallone. They were all there. All of them.

Jacob   They never fucking talked to us.

*As **Sarah** sings **Jacob** tries his hardest not to join in. He works hard cleaning up. Then getting himself ready to go and see **Marty**. But she seduces him into her song in the end.*

Sarah
   Do you remember our friend the doorman
   Who left nothing to chance
   He let in the rich and the famous
   But he loved the ones who came to dance

   Dance 'cause you're a lover
   Dance 'cause nothing's ever free
   Dance like you're pulled under water
   Dance like you drift in the sea

   Sha-ame is the enemy
   A sign your ghost is cold
   Dump the dust and
   Let 'em see ya
   Dance do what you're told

   Dance like it's all slipping through your hand

William
   Dance like you you never break a sweat

Jacob
   Dance like dancing in quicksand

Sarah
   Dance like you're hopelessly in debt

   Dance like a saint doing good deeds
   Throw those thighs around
   Love thy neighbor as thyself please
   Shake the fucking ground

John
   Dance like your life has been muted

Philip
   Dance like a pipe about to blow

   Drink from the skull of a cupid

Sarah
   Dance really put on a show

Dance like you burned all the prizes
No one hands to you
Find a fire who realizes
How tight they turn the screw

Jacob
Dance like you're running for your life

William
Dance like a chicken with no head

Jacob
Dance like the flash of a knife

William
Dance like you're better off dead

All
Dance!

Philip
Like you're climbing the walls

All
Dance!

Jacob
Like you're cursing at the gods

All
Dance!

John
Like they got you by the balls

All
Dance!

Misty
Like you're lonely as a dog

All
Dance!

Philip
Like an angel with a razor

All
Dance!

Misty
Like a vein that needs to bleed

All
Dance!

John
Like you're shot by a tazer

All
Dance!

William
Like pigs at their feed

All
Dance!

Sarah
Do 'the blind leads the blind'

All
Dance!

Misty
Like you're wiped off the map

All
Dance!

Sarah
'Cause maybe just maybe
The world doesn't give a crap

As the song gets wilder so the dance becomes more bacchanalian.

Patti *enters before the song finishes. She stands watching them dance for a while.*

Patti   Can you please keep the noise down?

Jacob   Patti.

William   Patti's here!

Sarah   Sweetheart, I'm sorry.

Patti   I don't mean to be a pain in the ass.

Jacob   You're not a pain in the ass.

Patti   I'm trying to sleep. I've got the exams tomorrow.

Jacob   I know, sweetheart.

Patti   I've been working my ass off for them.

Jacob   I know.

Sarah   We are dreadful people.

Patti   It's not that. It's just late.

Sarah   You're so much better than all of us.

Patti   I'm not saying that.

Sarah   And one day you will outgrow us.

Patti   It's not a question of outgrowing.

Sarah   And go and live in Europe. Or Asia. Or Africa.

Patti   I'm talking about the noise, nothing else.

Sarah   Or Antarctica. You will see the world.

Patti   Are you drunk?

Sarah   No. I'm not drunk. I'm happy is all. Happy to be alive in the face of this wondrous universe.

Misty   Patti, you should go to bed, honey. You've got a big day.

Patti   That's what I'm trying to do.

William   You're a good kid.

Sarah   She is so good.

William   Your dad's wrong about you.

Patti   What about me?

William   He's wrong to say he regrets having you.

Patti   What?

Jacob   I didn't say that.

William   He said that. That was his thing. He told me. I was telling him how great you girls are. He told me how you held him back, you 'restricted him'. He was talking about how great his life could have been if you'd never been born.

Jacob   William. No.

Patti   Did you say that?

Jacob   No I didn't.

William   He did.

Sarah   Patti, don't listen to him.

Jacob   You are a fucking piece of work.

Patti   Can I tell you? You are the worst thing that ever happened to me.

Philip   Patti, love, no.

Patti   You ruined my life when my mom left.

Misty   That's a bit melodramatic.

Patti   You're spending all the restaurant's money on things it can't afford so we're going to end up on the street.

Misty   Patti, come on.

Patti   And if that's not bad enough. You say that.

Jacob   I didn't.

Patti *leaves.*

Jacob Patti.

Misty I'll go.

Misty *follows her.*

Jacob Why did you do that?

William I was just telling the truth.

Sarah You wouldn't know the truth if it shat in your back seat.

She leaves to follow **Misty**.

Some time.

John Well. That was a rather remarkable ending to a rather remarkable day. In my opinion.

Philip Yes it was.

Some time.

John Even so.

Jacob What?

John All she does is sit in here all day. That can't be good for her. And it can't help with her education. Maybe you need to think about what kind of parent you want to be. Just a thought. I'll see you tomorrow.

Stunned they watch **John** *leave.*

Philip *clears up the glasses and the debris.*

William *watches him move.*

Philip *looks at him.*

Philip You're a classy guy, William. A real piece of work.

William Fuck you.

Philip In your dreams, cowboy.

He smiles at him. Leaves. **Jacob** *moves to* **William** *as though he's going to punch him.* **William** *grins.*

William   Oh I fucking dare you, dickwad! I fucking double dare you!

William *puts his hand on his pocket. There is a weapon in there. Maybe he gives* **Jacob** *just a little flash of it. It stops him in his tracks.*

Jacob   Was this what you wanted all along?

William   I seriously and honestly have no fucking idea what you're talking about.

Jacob   You can mess with me all you want but don't you dare bring my daughter into this.

William *is loving this.*

William   Can I get another Merlot, please?

Jacob   You told me you were going to be here at six.

William   Yeah?

Jacob   I'm supposed to be at this thing with Marty.

It's important.

William   Priorities. They're complicated things in my experience.

Jacob   I can't do it.

William   You can't do what?

Jacob   I stole from Marty. After everything he's done for me.

I can't do that and then sell the shit from here.

William   Sure you can.

Jacob   I can't, William. That's what I needed to tell you.

William   You can, baby.

Jacob   Don't call me baby.

William   It's easy.

Jacob   Not for me it's not.

William   I'm interested in your technique.

Jacob   My technique?

William   For initiating a transaction.

Jacob   It's not about the transaction.

William   Show me how you do it. Show me what you say to people. How you talk to them. We can fucking role-play.

Jacob   Don't mock me.

William   I'm not mocking you, Jacob, you fucking two bit schmuck.

Jacob   I need Marty's money back.

William   You what?

Jacob   The thousand dollars. I need the thousand dollars back.

William   Cute.

Jacob   I've still got all the shit.

William   Here's my thing. I needed a thousand dollars and I needed it fucking quickly. I knew where I could get it without even breaking into a sweat. I got it. Easy. Bingo. You were easy. Because you're a fucking clown.

Jacob   If Marty finds out what I've done I won't be able to look him in the eye.

William   It was gone in three hours.

We made a fucking deal. Next Tuesday, dickface. A week today. You owe me a thousand more.

Jacob   William, it's me.

William   Are you asking me to cut you some slack? Why because, what? You're scared all of a sudden?

Jacob   Because I'm your friend.

William   Wow.

Jacob   I've known you for ten years.

William   Your 'friend'?

Jacob   Sorry. That was a dumb thing to say.

William   No it wasn't. It was cute. I liked it. Just – Have you got the slightest idea what the fuck real life is like out there?

William
I live to be of service
I cannot pretend
And you shouldn't make me nervous
'Cause I'm not your friend

I'm the devil with the deal
I'm a wound that won't heal

I'm the knock knock knock on the door
The knock knock knock you've been waiting for

While you make your rukus
While you seal your fate
While you wait for justice
I'll clean your fucking plate

I'm the bullet you don't see
There's no bargaining with me

Do you think that you're immune
From the harm you do
All warm in your cocoon
Well I've got news for you

I'm the angel with the sword
I'm what can't be ignored

I'm the knock knock knock on the door
The knock knock knock you've been waiting for

Jacob   What are you going to do?

William   Use you fucking imagination. I'll see you next Tuesday.

William *leaves.*

Jacob *alone.*

He roars.

Sarah *comes back.*

Sarah   I have known men like him all my life. They are cancer.

I think I *might* be drunk actually.

Patti's fine. Thank you for asking. Misty's talking to her.

Jacob   Sarah, I don't have time for this. I gotta go and see Dan McCourt

Jacob *gets himself together to go out.*

Sarah   She's very important to me. Patti.

Jacob   I know that.

Sarah   This place is very important to me. If it closes, I have no idea what I will do.

She heads to the door. Looks around herself before she does.

There are so few other places I can afford to eat anymore!

She leaves.

He gets a jacket and puts it on. Tries to calm himself.

Misty *enters.*

Jacob   How's she doing?

Misty   She's okay.

Jacob   Thank you.

Misty   For what?

Jacob   For looking after her.

Misty   She's kind of my sister, kind of.

Jacob   Yeah.

I'm late.

You okay?

Misty   I'm alright.

He doesn't believe her. It makes him pause.

Jacob   There are so many things I want to say to you.

Misty   I know.

Jacob   I just can never find the, the the the the the –

Misty   A Tupperware box in the spice cabinet, Jacob? Seriously?

He stares at her. His world breaks a little.

She looks at him.

Misty   I found it when I was getting celery salt for the fucking Bloody Marys, you fucking piece of fuck.

Jacob   Misty.

Misty   Don't 'Misty' me, Jacob.

Jacob   William gave it to me to sell.

Misty   He did what?

Jacob   I am broke, Misty. I have been broke all my life. And I found a way to make some money for once and I never, like, I never have money. So I took it.

Misty   Jesus, Jacob.

Jacob   I got it from him for a thousand dollar advance that I stole from the till and I thought I could sell it but I can't. Not here. Not anywhere. He's given me a week. He's going to really hurt me, Misty. I have no idea what the fuck I am going to do.

He can't shake her gaze.

He leaves.

She is left alone.

Misty
Being loved as a child
Is like air or water or cigarettes
You basically need it to survive
And you don't need the regret

It's too much for anyone

All I wanted was a home
Life could finally be good
If you always burn your joy away
You're just a piece of wood

It's too much for anyone
For anyone for anyone

Act Four

A week later.

Mid-afternoon.

The restaurant is quieter.

Jacob *and* **Philip** *are finishing cleaning up after lunch and preparing for the evening.*

Jacob *and* **Philip**.

Jacob   I talked to Charlene.

Philip   Yeah?

Jacob   Yeah.

Philip   And?

Pause.

And, Jacob?

Jacob   She's gonna give up the lease.

Philip   Right. Cool. Fuck.

Jacob   Yeah.

Philip   When?

Jacob   As soon as she can by the sound of it. The place is gonna get sold to the first real estate developer they find.

Philip *looks at him.*

Philip   Did Daniel McCourt ever write back?

Jacob   Not yet. I'm gonna keep trying.

Philip *nods.*

Philip   How is Charlene?

Jacob   Like emotionally?

Philip   Yeah. Like emotionally.

Jacob   Bereft.

Philip   Have they got a date for the trial?

Jacob   For the cab driver?

Philip   Yeah.

Jacob   Not yet.

Philip   The piece of shit.

Jacob   I know.

Philip   The drunken incompetent lying malevolent shitball dirtbag piece of shit.

Jacob   He wasn't drunk. He'd been working twenty-seven hours straight. He hadn't slept in two days. He's twenty-two. He was trying to save money to go back home to Bolivia.

I was supposed to go with Marty. We were going to have a meeting with Daniel. I was supposed to be there. I would've been in the cab with him.

Philip *looks at him.*

Jacob   Philip?

Philip   Uh-huh?

Jacob   You seen Misty? It's been a week.

Philip   You know more than I do, Jacob.

They look at each other.

Jacob   She found out about the business with William. She found out I owed him money. It's gone. The stuff that I bought off William. It's gone.

Jacob *can't look at him.*

Philip   She's taken it.

Jacob *can't look at him.*

Philip   Jacob, she's taken it.

If she found the shit you left lying around, and it's fucking, what, disappeared? She's taken it and she's taken it to use it.

Sarah *enters. Sees the tension between* **Jacob** *and* **Philip**. *Chooses to say nothing about it. The briefest moment.*

Sarah   There is a patisserie on the corner of Carmine and 6th that is selling Edie Sedgwick Cupcakes. This is a city that has started to quote itself.

Good afternoon, gentlemen of my heart.

Jacob   Sarah.

Philip   Afternoon.

Sarah   You two seem to be enjoying a magnificent day in one another's company.

Jacob *and* **Philip** *don't shake eye contact.*

Jacob   The usual?

Sarah   Thank you, darling.

Jacob *leaves.*

Philip *pours her water.*

Philip   That man. Sometimes. He is one singular piece of work let me tell you that.

Sarah   You wanna know something surprising about him?

Philip   Jacob?

Sarah   Jacob.

He was the best lover I ever had.

He was much younger than me, but he was very attentive. He listened to me. And he had a beautiful cock. It was very smooth.

Philip   Smooth?

Sarah   Yeah. Smooth.

Jacob *enters. He has a glass of pastis.*

Jacob   Pastis

Sarah   Thank you, darling.

Jacob   Sure.

Jacob *is about to leave but* **Sarah** *drinks her drink in one go which rather surprises him and* **Philip**.

Sarah   To Marty.

The men nod.

Philip   Marty.

Jacob   Fuck, yeah.

Philip   Are you okay?

Sarah   I will miss him terribly.

Could I get my check, please?

Jacob   On the house.

She takes a moment to examine her surroundings.

Sarah   I had a vision. This afternoon.

Jacob   A vision?

Sarah   There's part of me that wonders if he sent it. It may have come from somewhere else altogether. I wanted to tell you about it.

Jacob   Excellent idea.

Philip *clears her glass. Smiles at* **Jacob**. *Leaves.*

Sarah   I needed to settle my nerves first.

Jacob   I'm sure you did.

Sarah   You know what I saw in this vision?

Jacob   I don't have a clue.

Sarah (*she speaks without pausing*)   I saw that this place will get sold and you and Patti will leave and I'll never see you again. Which is sad on one hand because I like your food and I like the people who work here. And on the other hand because this is the one place where I feel like I'm needed. And you, you are the one person who I ever wanted to need me.

And I know you will say something heroic and romantic now because you're kind of the heroic romantic type but it won't be truthful and if I had one wish for you, Jacob, before this place gets shat into the sewers of the city, it's that you try your hardest to tell the truth.

Sarah *kisses* **Jacob**.

'On the house'? No wonder you're closing down.

She leaves. **Jacob** *takes a moment then he leaves.*

The stage is empty for a while.

Jacob *enters.*

Daniel McCourt *enters.*

He is wearing a black running tracksuit and running shoes.

He has a biometric heart timer strapped to his arm which he fiddles with and occasionally checks.

Daniel   Jacob?

Jacob   Holy fuck.

Daniel   I – Er. I didn't mean to startle you.

Jacob   Daniel?

Daniel   Hi.

Jacob   Jesus H Christ on a freaking donkey. Come in. Come in. Come in man. Shit.

Daniel   It's been a while, huh?

Jacob   Yeah. Yeah. Yeah. I mean yeah. Yes, it has.

Daniel   I got your letters. I should have written.

Jacob   That's okay.

Daniel Then I heard about Marty.

Jacob Yeah.

Daniel It's awful.

Jacob Yes it is.

Daniel I thought I'd come by and see Charlene. I was in the – I was running. I was in the neighborhood. I should have gone home and changed. I was just passing down 7th. I should have changed. Maybe I'll go and change and come back.

Jacob No, Don't. It's fine. It'll be fine. You look fine. You look great.

Daniel I should have brought flowers.

Jacob No. You don't need to. She has plenty of flowers. Seriously. She doesn't need any more flowers.

Daniel Is she?

Jacob She's next door. Number 10. Apartment 6.

Daniel I thought they'd taken over this place.

Jacob They did. But they never actually lived here. I live back there still.

Daniel Right.

Jacob With Patti.

Daniel The kid you had with Crystal?

Jacob That's right.

Daniel Fuck. Is Crystal around?

Jacob No she's not.

Daniel Just the two of you?

Jacob Just the two of us.

Daniel   You're a single father, Jacob! That's immensely impressive. I always wanted kids. I never, er – It never –

Jacob   And Misty's here!

Daniel   Laura Hickman's daughter?

Jacob   She's staying at the moment. She's kind of like a sublet or a roommate or . . . I don't know.

This is very strange.

Daniel   Yeah. Yeah. Yeah. Yes, it is. How you doing, buddy?

Jacob   I'm – You know.

Daniel   Sure. Marty told me all about this place.

Jacob   Right.

Daniel   It's looking quiet, huh?

Jacob   Getting ready for the evening. You should have seen it last week. Seriously! It's been a strange couple of days.

Daniel   Grief is a profoundly dislocating process in my experience. You need to allow yourself to engage with it fully rather than trying to obstruct it or block it. The blockages will be damaging in the long run if you do that.

Jacob   What?

Daniel   Sorry. I have no idea why I said that. It's kind of strange being back here.

Jacob   It's not changed.

Daniel   No. It really hasn't. Those were some nights, huh?

Jacob   Yes they were.

Daniel   Some of the darkest nights of my life. Some of the bad times, you know?

There were times I woke up. I had vomit on my shirt. One time I pissed my pants. Did I ever tell you that?

Jacob   I'm not sure.

Daniel   I'm very ashamed. I look back on those nights and I feel very ashamed. You know what I mean?

Jacob   Sure.

Daniel   Kind of odd being back. Marty asked me to look into the place.

Jacob   I know that. That was what I was writing to you about.

Daniel   I arranged to meet him. I couldn't make it.

Jacob   That was where he was going.

Daniel *looks at him. Nods.*

Daniel   I thought about it. Looked at some of the margin reports he sent me. It's interesting when you contextualize them with developments in comparative areas in other parts of the city, you know? Thing about the restaurant industry is that the profit is never really in the food. Not really. You get two chefs, a bus boy, a dishwasher and three waiters and they don't clear anywhere near the profit that two barmen and a bar do in the same square footage. That's one thing you could do. Get rid of the food. Maybe do small plates. Tapas kind of thing. And just sell booze. Specialize. Become like a Russian tapas and vodka joint. Get a reputation that way. But around here? Even then. There's absolutely nothing going. The property value round Bleeker? The whole of the West Village? Absolutely no way. It's done. We're done. It's over. Red Hook looks good. Bushwick. Bits of Queens.

New York City, huh? It's how it all works.

Jacob   Right.

Daniel   The problem with a city that is built on newness is that it is always in a state of nostalgia because everything is always disappearing. 'Oh I miss the 90s. I miss the 70s. I miss the 50s. I miss fucking gaslight. They should never have built the park. They should never have designed the grid. They should never have gotten rid of the British. They should never have gotten rid of the Dutch. They should have never gotten rid of the Lenape Indians.'

Sorry.

I never got the chance to tell Marty that I wasn't going to help him. We were supposed to have a drink. I was gonna tell him that night. Which is –

Jacob   Yeah.

Daniel   I've been talking a hell of a lot. How are you, man?

Jacob   I'm good. I'm good.

Daniel   How old's Patti now?

Jacob   She's sixteen.

Daniel   How's her school going?

Jacob   It's good. It's good. It's great.

Daniel   I remember Crystal.

Jacob   I do too.

Daniel   She had an incredible energy. Beautiful eyes. Her hair! But it was her energy. It was like you were in the presence of something, you know? You still see any of the old crowd? Sarah still come in here?

Jacob   On occasion.

Daniel   Give her my love.

Jacob   I will.

Daniel   I might go and get changed before I go and see Charlene.

Jacob   Sure.

Daniel   Hey. Listen. Here's my number. We should get a coffee or something. I don't really drink a great deal these days. There are some non-alcoholic beers that are really great though. Or we could get a coffee. Catch up. I'd love to meet Patti one day.

Jacob   That would be great, Daniel. Man. I think about you a lot.

Daniel   You do?

Jacob   Sure. We were really hoping that thing might have worked out here.

Daniel   Yeah. It was never going to work out.

Would you forgive me? I really should go and see Charlene. Get changed. Get some flowers. I don't know. Text me, yeah?

Jacob   Sure. Sure.

Daniel   Number 10 right?

Jacob   Apartment 6.

Daniel   See you later.

Jacob   See you later, Daniel.

He leaves.

Jacob *watches him go.*

Nearly falls over. Stops himself.

Takes the dirty dishes to the back.

Misty *enters.*

Philip *enters.*

Misty   Hey.

Philip   Jesus Christ. Where have you been?

Misty   Oh. You know.

Philip   Shit.

Jacob!

Philip *leaves to get* **Jacob**.

Jacob *enters*.

They look at each other for a while.

Misty   I got you your money.

Jacob   You, what?

Misty   Here. It's mainly in small bills. Not for any reason. Other than. You know. The fucking world.

She gives him a paper bag full of money.

Jacob   Where have you been?

Misty   I've been selling your shit. You needed somebody to sell it. You looked kind of, what? Clueless? I figured if I told you, you would have tried to stop me. There are places I know that you would have no fucking idea about. So, I took it from you, and I sold it. I got you your money.

Jacob   I – I – I – I –

Are you okay?

Misty   Oh shit. Yeah. I'm fucking spectacular. How the fuck are you?

He looks at her.

He looks at the money. Tries not to.

Looks at her again.

Jacob   I don't know what to say to you.

Misty   There's thirteen hundred dollars there. I sold it at cost. I hope you don't mind. I wanted to move it quickly. You can keep the three hundred.

She leaves. But to the back of the restaurant not the street.

Jacob *looks at the bag. He takes out three hundred dollars and puts it in his pocket.*

Philip *enters.*

Jacob *looks at him.*

Philip   Are you okay?

Jacob   I think so.

Philip   Really?

Jacob   Sure. Sure. Sure.

Jacob *leaves.*

John *enters. He has an enormous armful of flowers.*

John   I followed her

I saw her. Coming out of the subway at West 4th. I followed her. Where is she?

Philip   Seriously?

John   Am I being ridiculous?

Philip   So ridiculous, Misty, honey!

He leaves. **Misty** *returns.*

John   Can I tell you something?

Misty   What?

John   I think you're not as bitter as you pretend to be. I think you carry all this bitterness with you and I think you're just pretending. You're not a bitter person. You're actually a kind person. And look. I know you have seen things and done things that are outside my own particular sphere of experience. And I have no idea where you have been for the last week. And I'm not sure I want to know, if I am really honest. You make me feel very naïve.

Misty   What do you want John?

John
  Finished my eggs
  Thought I was done
  Then you crashed the party
  Like fate had come

I've been waiting for
You to appear
I'm so glad we
Washed up here

I come here because
It's like being home
They hate what I do yet
Won't leave me alone

I've got to say it somehow
I've got to make it clear
We just had to
Wash up here

I'm not afraid
I have no fear
It had to be
We washed up here

Would you like these flowers?

She looks at them.

Examines them.

Misty   I mean.

Some time.

She takes them.

John   Thank you. That's a relief. That's good.

Misty   Thank you.

John   You should keep them in fresh water. Room temperature water if you can. There's a packet of protein that you can dissolve in the water. And you should keep them out of direct sunlight. I wanted you to have them. And if you ever I mean ever want to go and eat something. I would be honored to eat with you. I mean I know you kind of live in a restaurant so that might not be like the most exciting thing. But we could go to a different restaurant. Or a movie. Or the theater. Or have a drink. Or a walk.

Misty John.

John Or not. Let's not. It's a ridiculous idea.

Misty It's not.

John It is. It is. I'm very foolish. Keep the flowers.

Misty John. Not now. Not tonight. But one day. Another day. Maybe one day.

John Sure.

Misty I don't want to let you down.

John You are not. You're not. You're – Goodnight.

John *leaves.*

Philip *comes in.*

Philip We are going to put these in water.

Misty Thanks, Philip.

Philip Man oh man. This world.

He goes to leave and take the flowers.

She stops him.

Misty How did the Schenectady audition go?

Philip Oh. You know?

Misty You're still here?

Philip I still am.

Misty Right. Shit. I'm sorry.

Philip Could be worse. At least this place stops me from ever having to go back to Milwaukee.

Misty Fuck.

Philip Right.

Philip *leaves with the flowers.* **Jacob** *comes back.*

Misty   I heard about Marty.

Jacob   Yeah?

Misty   How old was he?

Jacob   He was my age.

Misty   That's fucked up.

What's going to happen?

Jacob   Charlene's going to give up the lease. She's going to get out of here.

Misty   What about Daniel McCourt?

Jacob   He never showed.

Misty   So are you going to need to look for somewhere else now too?

He can't answer.

You gonna leave the city?

Jacob   I don't know.

Po's closing.

Misty   Yeah.

Jacob   Taylor Swift's moving in right above it.

Misty   She's moving in fucking everywhere.

Jacob   Right.

Misty   If you did where would you go?

Jacob   I have no idea.

Misty   You could go back to Jersey City?

Jacob   I couldn't fucking bear that.

She's about to go. He stops her.

Jacob   I sometimes think about Pittsburgh.

Misty   There you go. Why Pittsburgh?

Jacob   I really – I like rivers. There's something about the idea of a city built on three rivers that's amazing to me. The world's largest bicycle museum is in Pittsburgh which I thought might be –

You ever get the feeling this whole country's had its time? We're running on fumes.

She doesn't answer.

Misty   I remember playing here when I was Patti's age. Younger maybe. Playing in the stairwell. In the lobby. You could get right into the alley and look up and see the moon.

Jacob   Your face. In the moonlight.

Misty   Do I look like Mom?

Jacob   I don't know, I can never figure that out. Yes. I mean yes. I mean of course you look like her.

Misty   I wondered.

Jacob   She was the love of my life, Misty. She got ill. There was nothing I could do for her anymore. But she was still the love of my life. Crystal came in here one night with Daniel McCourt. I slept with her once.

She got pregnant. I didn't know what to do. Laura couldn't handle it. I needed to look after Patti.

*It takes **Misty** some time to make sense of this.*

Misty   What happened to Crystal?

Jacob   She left.

Misty   Where is she now?

Jacob   The last she wrote she was upstate. But she moves around a lot. She meets these people. They have these ideas. They take her to different parts of the country. She follows them. She calls herself a 'seeker'. She promises that she's going to come and see Patti. Sometimes she does come. You never know when. It's a good trick.

William. He was going to hurt me, you know? You saved my life.

We've got a few weeks. I'll keep this place going until then. And I'll think about where we're going to go. If you want to stay here. For these weeks then, that would be. That would be good.

She looks at him. Smiles at him.

Misty
When a chef is cruel

Jacob
When he beats his eggs

Misty
You wanna hear our 'specials'

Jacob
He's serving you dregs

Misty
What if a chef

Jacob
Gets no rise from his dough

Misty
There's a friendly place

Jacob
Where bread makers go

Misty / Jacob
Pittsburgh
Pittsburgh

Jacob
The elegant citizens

Misty
With beautiful hair

Jacob
The cops only have

Misty
Hopes and a prayer

Jacob
And my god they even

Misty
Have better despair

Misty / Jacob
Pittsburgh
Pittsburgh

Misty
A town full of culture

Jacob
And sulphur and sin

Misty
By law you must smile

Jacob
But don't you dare grin

Misty
The river smells like blossoms

Jacob
Of a degenerate gin

Misty / Jacob
Pittsburgh
Pittsburgh

Cast
Pittsburgh

Jacob
Honest faces

Cast
Pittsburgh

Misty
Parking spaces

Cast
Pittsburgh

Jacob
Cleanest soap

Cast
Pittsburgh

Misty
Cries of hope

Cast
Pittsburgh

Jacob
Air is pure

Cast
Pittsburgh

Misty
Sidewalks sure

Cast
Pittsburgh

Jacob
Beauty sleep

Cast
Pittsburgh

Misty
Rents are cheap

Cast
Pittsburgh

Jacob
Friendly nurses

Cast
Pittsburgh

Misty
Empty curses

Cast
Pittsburgh

Jacob
Steepest street

Cast
Pittsburgh

Misty
Sandwich meat

Cast
Pittsburgh

Jacob
Good livin'

Cast
Pittsburgh

Misty
All forgiven

Cast
Where the truth sets you free!

Misty   I should get ready for the evening tables.

She leaves.

He is alone.

Jacob
Every day I do the daily grind
And it's for Patti so I don't mind

Half asleep doing time
So she can
Own the world

The truth in her face stops me dead
It shines one way: straight ahead
It kicks me in the balls and stomps on my head
She must own the world

I worry when she's grown up
She'll tell her shrink how I screwed up
And how I never showed up
She must own the world

Now the party's almost done
Maybe it's time to tell the truth and face the sun
Maybe if you have love then
You've won the world
Why not own the world
She must own the world

So every day I do the daily grind
And it's for Patti so I don't mind
I wake up resigned
That she will own the world
So she can own the world
Why not own the world

He sets about preparing the restaurant for one of the last few evening sittings.

William *enters.*

William   So?

Jacob   So.

William   How's Charlene?

Jacob   How do you think?

William   Right.

Jacob *hands* **William** *a bag of cash.*

Jacob   Here.

It's all there. You can count it.

William   I don't need to. I trust you.

If you ever wanted to sell some more.

Jacob   No.

William   You could.

Jacob   No.

William   Buy and sell keep the money moving. How this city works, Jacob.

Jacob   No.

William   How are you going to live, Jacob? You thought about where you're gonna go?

Jacob *doesn't answer.*

William   I just hope Patti's gonna be okay. I really like that kid. I've known her since she was six years old. Funny, huh?

Jacob *doesn't answer.*

William   I won't stay for a drink.

Jacob   No you fucking won't.

William   That's one thing I love about New Yorkers. They don't bullshit.

Jacob   William.

William   Chief?

Jacob   I'm a liar.

William   Cute.

Jacob   I have been a liar for much of my life.

William   Why are you still talking?

Jacob   I wanted to tell you the truth for once.

William   Why is he still talking?

Jacob   I used to think this city is built on people like you, you know? It really, really isn't.

William   I'll see you later.

Jacob   You are a blood sucking, soul-sucking, parasite cunt. You take and take and you give nothing and when you die, and you will die, you will die in pain and alone and screaming in fear and nobody will come and nobody will care and nobody will even notice.

William   Huh!

That was, that was really, that was mean, Jacob.

Cool.

Say goodbye to Misty. What kind of a fucking name is Misty?

William *leaves.*

Patti *enters.*

Jacob *continues his prepping.*

Patti   Hey.

Jacob   Yeah. Hey.

Patti   Has William gone?

Jacob   Just now.

Patti   He is such a creep.

Jacob   Yes he is.

Patti   'Parasite cunt.' Cool.

Misty's back.

Jacob   She is.

Patti   She staying?

Jacob   For a bit.

Patti   How long?

Jacob   I have no idea.

Patti   No. Cool.

I got my results. For the exams.

Jacob   What?

Patti   Today.

Jacob   Shit. I mean. How did you do?

Patti   I aced them. Straight As. I'm going to twelfth grade.

Jacob   Patti!

Patti   It's twelfth grade, Dad; it's not freaking Harvard. Please don't get weird.

Jacob   Baby!

Patti   Oh God, please don't.

Jacob   You showed them, babe.

Patti   You helped.

Jacob   How?

Patti   You know.

I mean you let Misty stay in my fucking room so I had to stay at school and work so I could concentrate more, I guess.

Nothing else. Honestly.

Jacob   Patti.

Patti   What?

Jacob   Don't curse. Not right in front of me.

Patti   Sorry, Dad.

Jacob   That's okay. You're a punk. You can't help it.

Patti   I'm not a punk.

Jacob Patti Smith that's who you were named after.

Patti I know Dad, Jesus.

Jacob You telling me that Patti Smith is not a punk?

Patti How many times have I heard this story? Just because the person you named me after was a punk doesn't mean I am a punk. We are entirely different people.

Jacob I am so proud of you.

Patti You said. Please don't go on about it.

Jacob I won't. I promise.

Patti Dad, can I ask you a question?

Jacob Sure thing, kiddo.

Patti What do you think happens when you die?

Jacob I have no idea.

Patti It was a bit of a long shot, I have to admit.

I don't think Mom is gonna come this month, do you?

Jacob I don't know. If I know anything about your mom it's that she will always take me by surprise.

Patti I don't know if I can take her doing this to me. Letting me down. When I need her. Is that a terrible thing to say?

Jacob No.

Patti What do you think I should do, Dad?

Jacob I think you should know that you can live without her perfectly well.

Patti Sure.

Jacob And that sometimes she will come back. And sometimes she won't. But neither time is it your fault. It's her. Not you. You need to be able to tell her to fuck herself when you need to. You need to be as honest as you can.

Patti   That's rich coming from you.

Jacob   I know that.

Patti   When we leave here where are we gonna go?

Jacob   I don't know.

Patti   Probably leave New York though, right?

Jacob   I think we will, Patti, yeah. I think we will.

Patti   I wouldn't mind that. I just want to live somewhere normal. Like in a house not in a bar.

Can I ask you another question?

Jacob   Sure.

Patti   Do you really regret having me? Please be honest, please. I really need you to be honest with me.

Jacob *sings 'So Easy to Love' to her.*

Jacob
    The first time I saw you
    I finally understood
    That love is a law that binds you
    Like you hoped it would

    For you I live every day
    My heart holds your pain
    No matter what you do or say
    You'll flow through my veins

    You can lose it all trying to get lucky
    But you're my luck you're the fate that saves me

    Hope you can love this sad old clown
    Remember love isn't pity
    Love is a magic that I just believe
    Like a fool in love with New York City

For a complete listing of
Methuen Drama titles, visit:

www.bloomsbury.com/drama

Follow us on Twitter and keep up to date
with our news and publications

@MethuenDrama